Copyright © 2023 Author Name Louise Cowley

ISBN: 9798802537541

THE SHROUD: THE EVIDENCE

The Shroud

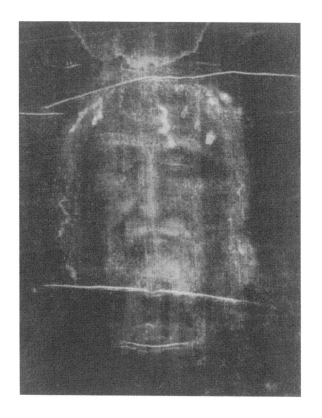

The Evidence

LM Cowley

THE SHROUD: THE EVIDENCE

Table of Contents

THE SHROUD: THE EVIDENCE

Introduction

By studying the data available that has been accumulated objectively from the scientists on the STURP (Shroud of Turin Research Project) team and those who have followed on with research on the Shroud, a clear and unbiased understanding can be gained. This can then be compared with the opposing view. The question may be asked: Can any of these claims be refuted from the scientific data available and do these opinions contain any bias?

Dr Eric Jumper, the vice-president of the STURP team, stated that his personal view was that the Shroud probably was not authentic as it seemed too good to be true. Nevertheless, he recognized that research had not come up with anything that eliminated the possibility that it was.

Jumper spoke of how the media had attacked the credibility of the scientists rather than attacking the data they produced. The only reason for this seemed to be that the data contradicted what they believed was the cause of the image; in other words, their opinion of the Shroud's authenticity biased them against the facts.

Jumper added: "All we have done is provided a discriminating set of data. We're not trying to grind any axes." [1]

The Shroud remains a controversial subject. It is rarely seen with objective eyes but has become something of a symbol for belief in Jesus Christ as the Son of God (perhaps more so for the sceptics). Anti-authenticists are often vehemently opposed to entertaining the notion that it could be genuine as they cannot reconcile this with the idea that Jesus of Nazareth might have been a real person. It seems too much to admit he may have existed.

This is not to say that everyone thinks in this way, but it has to be said there are people on both sides of the spectrum that take their personal beliefs to extremes; ; the important thing is to try and look at the evidence with an open mind and then draw your own conclusions. The rest is down to faith.

Part 1- A Debated History

The Shroud of Turin is the most famous and most mysterious relic of Christ and reveals a ghostly and beautiful image that seems to hover in front of the cloth but is, in fact, part of the cloth.

This was not buried with the cross of Christ but found in a corner of the tomb after the Resurrection as is written in the Bible. It disappeared after this and was not one of the relics discovered by St Helena.

Despite being declared a medieval forgery, there is still no explanation for how the image was formed and no replication of it so far. But what is its mysterious history? If it is indeed the genuine burial cloth, then where did it disappear to after its discovery in the tomb?

Ian Wilson, author of the best-selling book, *The Shroud of Turin*, argues that the Shroud had been documented before its first official date of

1355, as the 'Image of Edessa 'and the 'Holy Mandylion'. In the *Story of the Image of Edessa,* the cloth is said to have been mounted on a board as a portrait of the face.[2]

Author, Ian Wilson, believes that this was the Shroud, doubled and folded in four- described as 'tetradiplon '(doubled in four) in the Acts of Thaddeus.[3]

A 10th-century codex was found in the Vatican Library which contained an 8th-century account of an imprint of Christ's body on a canvas kept in a church in Edessa. It quotes a man called Smera from Constantinople: "King Abgar received a cloth on which one can see not only a face but the whole body" (in Latin: [non tantum] faciei figuram sed totius corporis figuram cernere poteris) [4]

Mark Guscin writes in his book on the Image of Edessa:

'...it should be stressed that there are no artistic representations of the Image of Edessa as a full-body image or with bloodstains, and the majority of texts make no reference to either characteristic; but at the same time it is undeniable that at some point in the history of the Image of Edessa, some writers were convinced, for whatever reason, that it was indeed a full-body image on a large cloth that had been folded over (possibly in such a way that only the face was visible), and that it did contain bloodstains. '[5]

There is a legend that the burial linens of Jesus were taken to Edessa, (now known as Şanliurfa in south-eastern Turkey) sometime during the first century. Through this, King Abgar V, a contemporary of Jesus, was converted to Christianity. After his death, his son reverted to paganism and the Shroud is thought to have been hidden in the city walls for its own protection and to protect the city against invaders.

There is no mention of the Shroud in Edessa until the 6th century when Evagrius Scholasticus, a Syrian scholar, recorded an attack between the Edessans and Persians. In this chronicle, he wrote of the 'Image of Edessa 'which was said to protect the Edessans, describing it as:

11

'the divinely created Image, which human hands had not made (acheiropoietos), the one that Christ the God sent to Abgar when he yearned to see him.' [6]

At this time, it was clearly believed to not be a painting, but an image given by God. It may well have been rediscovered in 525 AD when the flooding of Edessa killed as many as 30,000 people and required many buildings to be reconstructed. This included the city walls.

Around this time, there was also a change in the way Jesus was depicted in art. In the early centuries, he was mainly shown to be beardless but from the 6th century onwards, Jesus is often portrayed in a frontal position with long hair and a long nose, resembling the image shown on the Shroud.[7]

Coincidence or not? And if the discovery of the Shroud did not prompt this change, then what did?

Christ Pantocrator icon, preserved in the remote monastery of St Catherine in the Sinai desert (6th century)

Relief portrait of Christ on a silver vase found in Syria, now in the Louvre in Paris (late 6th- Early 7th century)

Although Edessa had a strong Christian community, its citizens had accepted the rule of Arab Muslim overlords since 639 AD. However, in 943 AD, the Arab rulers of Edessa were confronted with an 80,000 strong Byzantine army led by the Christian general, John Curcuas. He offered the Muslim emir a deal. He would spare the city, giving it perpetual immunity, release 200 Muslim prisoners they held and offer a huge sum of money: all for the Image of Edessa. After much haggling, it was handed over despite opposition from the Christian community and transported from Edessa to Constantinople in the year 944 AD. [8]

14

The Image of Edessa was first taken to the Blachernae church, then on to the Pharos Chapel in the Great Palace (now known as Hagia Sophia), where it was housed with many illustrious relics of the Passion, including part of the title that had been on the Cross.[9] In Constantinople, it became known as the 'Holy Mandylion 'and stayed there for almost two and a half centuries until the devastating Fourth Crusade, which took place between 1202 and 1204 AD.

The intention behind the Fourth Crusade led by Pope Innocent III, was to take back Muslim-controlled Jerusalem by means of an invasion through Egypt. Instead, the Crusaders diverted to Constantinople to restore the Byzantine prince, Alexios Angelos. The Crusaders, unpaid by the Byzantines for their services, took matters into their own hands and in their greed, completely looted and destroyed Constantinople, committing violent, atrocities of war. It caused a major rift between Orthodox and Catholic Christians that is not forgotten, even today. [10]

An ordinary soldier, named Robert de Clari, had seen the burial shroud of Jesus in Constantinople and wrote the following words:

"There was another church which was called My Lady St Mary of Blachernae, where there was the shroud, where there was the sydoine* in which Our Lord had been wrapped, which every Friday stood upright, so that one could see the figure of Our Lord on it."

Although the cloth would have normally been kept in the Pharos chapel, in times of danger, it was taken to the Blachernae church to invoke protection over the city. During the Sack of Constantinople, the Shroud disappeared and although Robert de Clari made specific enquiries as to its whereabouts, he wrote, **"No one, either Greek or French, ever knew what became of this sydoine when the city was taken."** [11]

The Image of Edessa disappeared in 1204 and the Shroud surfaced in France during the 1350s, now owned by the knight, Geoffrey de

Charney. Could they have possibly been one and the same thing?

If so, what happened to it in this interim period lasting 150 years?

Geoffrey I de Charny of Lirey was the first recorded owner of the Shroud in the west. He is thought to be related to another Geoffrey de Charny, a Templar Knight burned at the stake in 1314 with another Templar, Jacques de Molay. Their crime was heresy, an accusation they both denied.

Although no one knows if these claims were true, the French King, Philip the Fair, certainly had sufficient, personal reason to get rid of them as he owed them a great deal of money. The Templars were a Catholic military order founded in 1119 and were known for their secret, ritualistic practices. They were said to worship a 'bearded head'. What this was exactly is not known but the French Templar knight, Arnaut Sabbatier, wrote of, 'a secret place to which only the brothers of the Temple had access 'and was shown, 'a long, linen cloth on which was imprinted the figure of a man.'[12]

During World War II, a panel painting was discovered in the ceiling of a cottage in Templecombe after some plaster fell down. It was a bearded face that appeared to be the head of Christ but without any halo and similar to copies of the Image of Edessa and the face on the Turin Shroud.

The wood it was painted on, dated from 1280 to 1310 and from 1185 until the 14th century, Templecombe had been an important training ground for the Templar Knights. [13] It may well be that the Shroud had been in this location, or the painting had been made by someone who had seen the Shroud first-hand.

1355 was the first public showing of the Shroud and one single, surviving example of a souvenir badge of this occasion still exists today. It depicts the Shroud in its full-length, double-imprint form, the earliest surviving work of art to show it in this way.[14]

Lead pilgrim's badge or medallion in the Cluny Museum, Paris from the first undisputed exposition of the Shroud at Lirey, France from c.1355-56.

For Shroud sceptics, its history begins around the year 1355, the first date it was documented and well within the dates given by the carbon-14 test results of 1988. It sounds very plausible that it could be a medieval forgery on a very simplistic level; but the Shroud is much more complicated and mysterious than that.

A picture exists that is dated well before this, between 1192 and 1195 and appears to portray the Shroud. It is called the Pray Codex, commonly referred to as the Hungarian Pray Manuscript, a collection of medieval manuscripts named after György Pray, who discovered it in 1770.

One of its illustrations depicts the burial and resurrection of Jesus with certain similarities to the Shroud.

The Pray Codex

Jesus is shown to be naked with his arms crossed at the pelvis, noticeably only revealing four fingers without thumbs as on the Shroud. There is a clear blood mark on his forehead also apparent on the Shroud with other marks appearing on his head. However, perhaps the most interesting feature is the representation of the herringbone weave of the cloth by the artist and what appears to be the L-shaped pattern of burn holes found on the cloth. All these features combined seem too specific to be mere coincidence and it would appear that the artist had seen the Shroud during the 12th century and copied it. The Gregory Sermon of 944, also suggests the arrival of a cloth in Constantinople from Edessa. Gregory, the Archdeacon of Hagia Sophia in Constantinople is quoted as saying,

"By the simple touching to the face of Christ, an image of his form was made..." [15]

LOCATIONS OF THE SHROUD AFTER 1355

The first known owner of the Shroud was a knight named, Geoffrey (Geoffroi) I de Charny who is believed to have acquired it as 'spoils of war 'in Constantinople. In 1355, there was an exposition of the Shroud held in Lirey, in France and special souvenir medallions were struck. One year later, De Charny was killed in battle and the Shroud remained in his family at Lirey. Margaret de Charny is recorded as exhibiting the Shroud in Liège and Germolles, near Mâcon in France. At some time, probably during the early 1450s, it passed from her ownership to Duke Louis I of Savoy. In 1502, the Shroud was transferred to the Sainte Chapelle at Chambéry where a fire, (1532), caused the silver reliquary to melt causing holes and scorch marks in the Shroud but not seriously damaging the image. The Shroud was moved around and exhibited in different places and spent 20 years in Vercelli in northern Italy before being brought to Turin in 1578. It was taken to an abbey, north-east of Naples for safety during the Second World War and returned to Turin in 1946 where it has been ever since. In 1983, the ex-king of Italy, Umberto II, died and bequeathed the Shroud to the Pope and his successors with the proviso that the cloth is to always stay in Turin.[16]

THE SHROUD: THE EVIDENCE

THE FIRST PHOTOGRAPH OF THE SHROUD- 1898

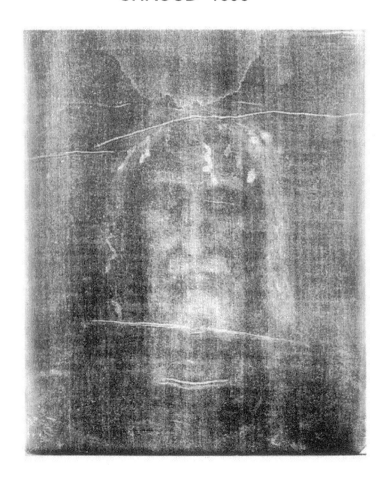

Pia Secondo, the photographer of the Shroud, pictured right

Historical records and images from the past can piece together parts of the puzzle and examine most likely scenarios. However, it is science that has unlocked some of the cloth's greatest mysteries and continues to do so today. This is seen firstly with photography when on May 28th, 1898 in Turin, permission was given to photograph the Shroud for the first time, during one of its rare expositions.

26

Pia Secondo, the official photographer, almost dropped the glass plate in the darkroom as the clear and detailed image appeared before his eyes.

The image on the glass plate appeared as a perfect positive of a man composed solemnly in death. In other words, the form on the cloth itself was the perfect negative of this developed likeness. The details of the face and body only become clearly recognizable when viewed in photographic negative.

Father Antonio Tonelli wrote in an Italian publication in 1929: "Pia told a friend of mine that once (he) placed the plate in the bath, he felt the need to jump because he was so filled with emotion and happiness."[17]

The other detail is remembered by an assistant of Pia's nephew:

"Pia was at the threshold of the darkroom. In his hands he held the big plate still dripping fixative. Once close to him, my grandfather was struck by the strange expression of his

THE SHROUD: THE EVIDENCE

face. He looked down at the plate and saw…"
[18]

Pia later recalled: "Shut up in my darkroom, all
intent on my work, I experienced a very strong
emotion when, during the development, I saw
for the first time the Holy Face appear on the
plate, with such clarity that I was dumbfounded
by it…".[19]

The shock and realization of what the image on
the Shroud signified, meant that the owner of
the Shroud, the King of Italy, decided to
withhold information from the public while he
discussed the implications with his advisors.
The news leaked out anyway. Newspapers
around the world revealed this exciting
discovery although the only photographs that
were printed of the image were of low quality in
two magazines. It made no difference; the
public was fascinated.[20]

As is often the case, the Shroud was taken as
being incredible, in the non-believing sense.
Controversy was directed towards Pia
Secondo who was accused of fraud and
trickery in the darkroom. Despite his opponents
knowing little about photography, they accused

28

him of overexposing the plate to create the image (not possible) and of creating a transparency, which would require the red silk lining to be taken off the back of the Shroud. Neither of these accusations were true.

Secondo was surprised and distressed at these reactions to his work and appealed to Professor Porro, an expert in analytical chemistry, who assured him he had done nothing wrong. His final vindication, however, came in 1931 when he was in the audience to witness the results of Giuseppe Enrie's photographs of the Shroud which produced exactly the same negative image... as expected.[21]

1898 exhibition in the cathedral- photograph by Pia Secondo

Part 2- The Forensic Examinations of the Photograph of the Shroud

With the advent of photography in the 19th century, scientific study of the Shroud was able to begin. The sudden appearance of detailed photographs meant that medical experts could now closely examine the wounds of crucifixion and scourging.

YVES DELAGE AND PAUL VIGNON (1902)

Paul Vignon was a biologist who worked with Yves Delage, a professor of anatomy at the Sorbonne in Paris. Delage believed that the photographs of the Shroud were anatomically correct and could not have been produced by an artist. Encouraged by his mentor, Vignon conducted experiments to prove this hypothesis which included testing paint on linen and seeing that when the material was rolled up, the paint cracked, something that did not happen with the Shroud. The use of dye was also discounted as the liquid would have spread along the threads. Vignon believed the Shroud image was produced by vaporization and tried to reproduce the image using various means but was unable to do so. He became convinced it was authentic, as did Delage.

In 1902, Delage spoke of their findings at the Paris Academy of Sciences, the same year Paul Vignon published his book on the Shroud. Delage explained that due to the wounds being anatomically correct, this excluded the possibility that the Shroud was the work of a forger. He was unpleasantly taken aback by how his findings were received. The Academy refused to print any part of Delage's paper that indicated the image on the Shroud was that of Jesus Christ. His presentation was met with such controversy that Delage soon gave up his studies on the Shroud.

Delage wrote to the editor of Revue magazine. The letter is as follows:

"When I paid you a visit in your laboratory several months ago to introduce you to Vignon... had you the presentiment of the impassioned quarrels which this question would arouse...?

I willingly recognize that none of these given arguments offer the features of an irrefutable demonstration, but it must be recognized that their whole constitutes a bundle of imposing probabilities, some of which are very near being proven... a religious question has been needlessly injected into a problem which in itself is purely scientific, with the result that feelings have run high, and reason has been led astray. If, instead of Christ, there were a question of some person like a Sargon, an Achilles or one of the Pharoahs, no one would have thought of making any objection... I have been faithful to the true spirit of science, in treating this question, intent only on the truth, not concerned in the least whether it would affect the interests of any religious party... I **consider the Christ to be an historical**

33

personage and I do not see why anyone should be scandalized that there exists a material trace of his existence." [22]

There are similarities between this situation and how the STURP team's data was viewed. Both Delage and the scientists of 1978 were examining the Shroud scientifically and both were surprised by how the religious arguments concerning the Shroud caused many to disregard their findings through prejudice.

Also in 1902, after careful study of the first photograph of the Shroud, Vignon published his first book: 'The Shroud of Christ', afterwards remaining silent on this subject for nearly thirty years. During the Shroud exhibition of 1933, he was one of the few scientists admitted, for one whole night, to scrutinize the relic in minute detail. From this, he wrote, 'The Holy Shroud of Turin: Science, Archeology, History, Iconography, Logic ' (1938) for which the French Academy awarded him a prize.

One of Vignon's main contributions to Shroud research was his identification of similarities

34

between portraits of Christ from the 6th century onwards and the Shroud of Turin. Whereas before this time, Jesus was mainly portrayed as beardless, after the 6th century certain standard features began to appear on likenesses of Christ which were comparable to the features seen on the Shroud. Vignon made particular note of fifteen features on the face of the image that have come to be known as the 'Vignon markings'. These were then used to identify similar features in early paintings and representations of Jesus. Ian Wilson continued with this area of research, believing that the Shroud, (thought to be the Mandylion), was folded in such a way that only the head was visible and was consequently depicted this way in art.

The cloth may have been presented this way in order to hide the blood and the nakedness of the body.

Prof. Yves Delage 1854-1920

Prof. Paul Vignon 1865-1943

DR PIERRE BARBET (1950)

The Shroud was displayed publicly in 1931 in honor of the wedding of Umberto II to the Belgian princess Maria José and a new set of photographs were commissioned by professional photographer, Giuseppe Enrie. Accompanied by Secondo Pia, a French scientist and a priest, Enrie made twelve negatives of the Shroud. These photographs were of a much higher quality than the original pictures of 1898 as in the interim, there had been great advances in photographic techniques, and he was permitted to photograph the Shroud without its glass cover. Enrie photographed the complete Shroud as well as life-size close-ups of the face, the back and the shoulders and also of the bloodstain on the wrist area of the left arm.[23]

Dr Pierre Barbet (1884-1961) was a French Physician, chief surgeon general and a pioneer in the field of crucifixion and Shroud research. He used Giuseppe Enrie's photographs of the Shroud to provide a forensic pathologist's analysis of the wounds seen on the cloth and wrote about this and theories on the crucifixion of Jesus in his book, 'A Doctor at Calvary ' (1950). Barbet believed that the Shroud was authentic, anatomically correct and consistent with crucifixion and drew upon experiments and his experience as a battlefield surgeon during World War I to support this.

Barbet mounted and nailed an amputated arm through the palm, to a piece of wood, attaching a 100lb weight. It took only 10 minutes before the wound had become a gaping hole. With one shake, the palm burst open and fell to the floor. This experiment on a cadaver led him to search for a place within the wrist that would hold a crucified body in place until death occurred. Barbet believed this place to be an area in the wrist called 'Destot's Space 'not far from the little finger. He thought the missing thumb on the Shroud was due to injury to the median nerve by the passage of the nail. However, it was later shown that the median nerve would not have been damaged if a nail had passed through this area. Dr Frederick Zugibe (1928-2013), professor of pathology and one of the United States 'most prominent forensics experts, conducted experiments that showed it was far more likely the nail had passed through the wrist area close to the thumb where the median nerve would still have been damaged and is consistent with the image of the four fingers and no visible thumb on the Shroud.

Pierre Barbet saw the Shroud of Turin the last time it was shown outside on the steps of the Cathedral of Saint John the Baptist on Sunday October 15, 1933.

"I was in front of them, on the cathedral steps, and His Eminence, Cardinal Fossati, Archbishop of Turin, very kindly placed the frame on the edge of the steps for a few minutes, so that we could have a good look at it. The sun had just gone down behind the houses on the other side of the square; the bright but diffused light was ideal for observation. I, therefore, saw the Shroud in broad daylight, uninterrupted by glass, at a distance of less than a meter, and suddenly I experienced one of the strongest emotions of my life. For I saw, without expecting it, that all the wound images were of a clearly different color from the body as a whole; and this color was of that of dried blood having impregnated the cloth."

It was not until the 1970s that proof was established that the Shroud contained real blood. Pierre Barbet could see this clearly without needing any proof. He wrote that on the steps the crowd broke into applause. "As for me, a Catholic and a surgeon, my soul was overwhelmed by this sudden revelation, and enthralled by this real presence which was inescapably self-evident to me, I went down on my knees and adored in silence. ☐"[24]

Dr Pierre Barbet 1884-1961

DR ROBERT BUCKLIN (1970)

1916-2001

Dr Robert Bucklin, an expert in forensic pathology, found much evidence to show that the cloth had indeed covered the body of a scourged and crucified man. He was also a member of the STURP team who studied the photographs after the scientific examination but was not personally present in Turin. In the Bafta-winning documentary, *Silent Witness* (1977), he is seen performing a forensic examination using life size photographs of the Shroud. A summary of his findings are as follows taken from the paper, *The Legal and Medical Aspects of the Trial and Death of Christ* by Robert Bucklin, M.D., J.D. (Medicine, Science and the Law, 1970) [25]

The cloth is remarkable because on it there is imprinted an image of a human body showing frontal and dorsal views. Present also on the cloth are blood stains, marks left by fire, and some large water stains. The cloth was first photographed in 1898 by Secondo Pia and again in 1931 by Giuseppe Enrie. The photographs of Enrie are remarkable for their clarity and it is the study of these photographs, including life-size enlargements, which are the basis of my medical interpretation of the events of the Crucifixion.

The imprint of the body image shows an adult male about 5'11" in height and weighing approximately 175 pounds, estimated to be between 30-35 years of age.

The stiffness of the extremities in the imprints is strongly suggestive that rigor mortis had taken place. The image on the Shroud is effectively a mirror image with right and left reversed, but when shown as a negative, the man can be seen more clearly and is not reversed. The injuries to the body can be best divided into five groups: The marks of the scourge, the nail imprints in the wrists, the nail marks in the feet, the wounds on the head, and the wound in the chest.

1. THE MARKS OF THE SCOURGE AND THE ABRASIONS

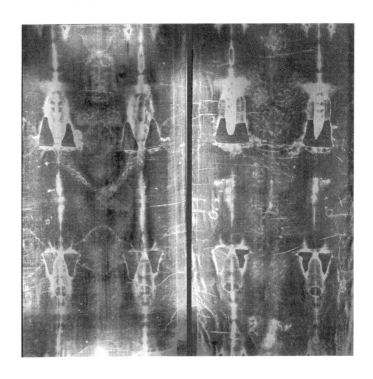

The marks of the scourge appear on the front and back of the body but are most distinct over the back. Here they extend from the shoulders down as far as the calves of the legs. On the front of the body, they also appear on the chest and legs, but there is no evidence of marks of the scourge on the arms or forearms. From this fact it may be assumed that the arms were elevated over the head at the time of the scourging. The scourging was done as a preliminary to the crucifixion, and according to historians, it was a common event. The implement used was a whip-like structure called a flagrum. It consisted of two or three thongs, at the ends of which were tied small bits of either bone or metal. The implement was applied to the body in such a way as to produce bleeding by the metal or bone tearing the skin. The marks, as they appear on the Shroud image, clearly define the shape of the tip of the flagrum. It is notable that the imprints of the scourge appear in a sheaf-like fashion directed downward and medially from the shoulders. Their appearance would serve to indicate that there were either two persons doing the scourging or that one person changed his position from the right to the left side. The number of scourge marks is particularly interesting. It was the Jewish law that the scourging would be limited to forty blows, and, as a matter of habit, the limit was practically set at thirty-nine. Scourging under the Roman law, as occurred in the case of Christ, was unlimited in its extent and those who have counted the scourge-mark images on the Shroud have variously estimated them to be as many as one hundred.

THE ABRASIONS FROM THE CROSS

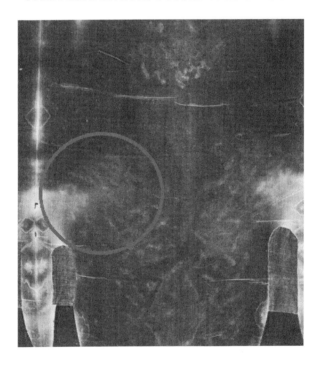

From an examination of the imprint of the back, it is possible to draw some conclusions as to the structure and manner of carrying the cross. It is highly improbable that Christ carried his entire cross, supported over one shoulder as it would have been an extremely heavy structure, estimated to have weighed nearly 300 pounds. It is doubtful that anyone could have carried this weight even for six hundred yards. Since crucifixion was a common method of putting victims to death, the upright portion of the cross, known as the stipes, was permanently in place at the point of execution. It was a long beam firmly embedded in the ground and extending up for about eight feet. The crossbar or patibulum was the portion carried by the victim. The weight of the crosspiece is unknown but has been estimated to weigh as much as eighty pounds. The manner in which the patibulum was supported on the body appears definite by examination of the imprints of the back on the Shroud. Had the crossbar been carried over one shoulder, it could reasonably be expected that it would have produced a large bruise on the shoulder. Since all the other bruises suffered by Christ during his Passion have appeared so distinctly on the

Shroud image, one wonders why there is no evidence of a bruise on the shoulder. However, examination of the back in the region of the scapulae shows two large areas of bruising. These might have been produced by the crossbar being supported over the upper portion of the back rather than being balanced on one shoulder. A weight thus supported is easier to carry, since it is divided over a large area.

Two areas of abrasion were discovered on the shoulder blades, caused by a heavy object resting on the back. Crucifixion victims would carry the crossbeam attached to the shoulders with rope, to the place of execution. There, it would be attached to the stipe, a wooden beam permanently fixed into the ground.

Another explanation for these bruises might be the writhing of the victim while suspended on the cross.

Over 120 strokes with double puncture-type wounds, were counted on the image of the body, believed to have been caused by two flagrams, one from the left and one from the right.

1. THE WOUNDS ON THE HEAD AND THE FACE

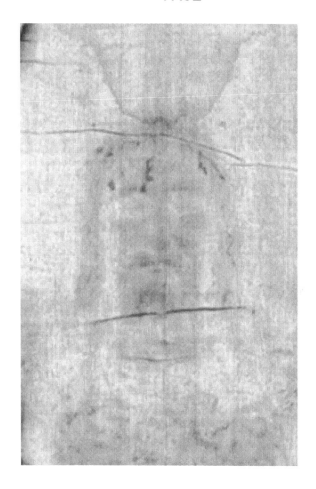

The cloth of the Shroud

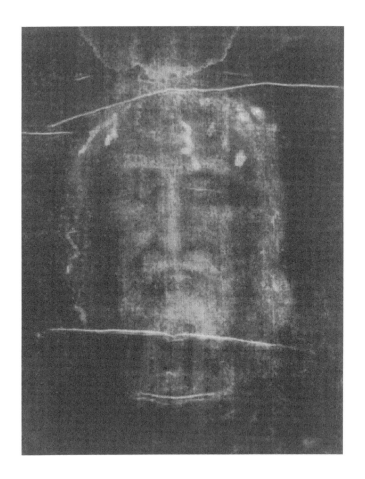

Negative of the Shroud

The face of the Shroud shows a partial closing of the right eye and a swollen right cheek. The nose appears fractured and there is an abrasion on the tip, perhaps caused by a fall when the nose came into contact with a hard object. The left leg also has lacerations resulting from a fall.

Bright red blood stains, seen on the forehead and the scalp were found to contain traces of bilirubin, a substance produced by the liver when the body is under severe trauma. It contains an orange/yellow pigment that causes the blood to remain this color instead of changing to dark brown.

These stains were caused by sharp pointed objects projected below the skin, like a cap that rested on the head.

This wound corresponds to the crown of thorns. This more than anything else, identifies the man as Jesus Christ as this torture was reserved for him and him alone. It was not normal Roman procedure to crown the victim with thorns and a forger would have included some wounds but would have more than likely portrayed it as a circlet rather than a clump of thorns.

The marks on the head constituted the third group of injuries. On the front of the face, in the forehead, there are several blood prints. One of these has the shape of a figure 3. On the back of the head, circling the scalp, is another row of blood prints. These were left by the crown of thorns. High on the scalp are similar blood stains which can be explained if one assumes that the crown of thorns, instead of a circlet, was shaped more like a cap and that there were branches and thorns laced over the top of the cap. The thorns were of the Zizyphus spina species and were approximately one inch in length. Passing through the skin and subcutaneous tissues of the scalp, they lacerated vessels and as is well known of scalp injuries, there was a considerable amount of bleeding because of the retraction of the torn vessels. On the face, corresponding to the right cheek, there is a swelling of the malar region which has resulted in partial closure of the right eye. Presumably this injury occurred during the time of the trial in the courtyard of Caiaphas, when it is recorded that Christ was struck in the face by one of the soldiers. There is a very slight deviation of the nose, possibly reflecting a fracture of the nasal cartilage. At the tip of the nose there is a bruise which may have occurred during one of the falls while carrying the cross. A small moustache is readily visible on the upper lip, and covering the chin is a short beard which is divided into two portions. The straightness of the sides of the face and the separation of the locks of hair from the face are accounted for by a chin band which was placed around the jaw and over the top of the head.

2. THE NAIL IMPRINTS IN THE WRISTS

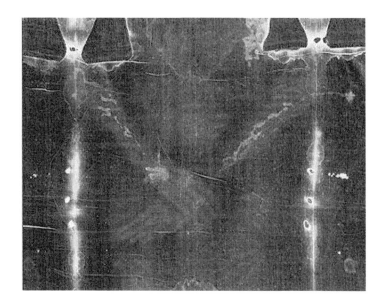

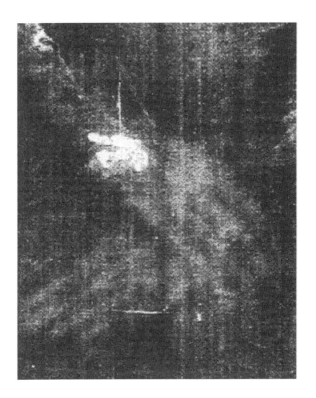

On the left wrist is a puncture-type wound. An injury in the wrist will penetrate the median nerve which functions to flex the thumb across the palm. There are no thumbs in this image.

Examination of imprints left by the hands and arms of Christ provides a great deal of information, and here again it becomes immediately apparent that the position of the nails as ordinarily depicted is subject to some question.

The hands as they appear on the imprint, show the marks of four fingers well. There is, however, no evidence of imprints left by the thumbs. The hands are crossed, with the left hand appearing on top of the right and covering the right wrist. In the region of the left wrist, there is a bloodstain which represents the mark left by the nail. That this mark is not in the palm is easily ascertained by simple measurements taken from the site of the mark to the tips of the fingers, proving that the mark is not in the center of the palm, but in the wrist. The mark left by the nail in the right wrist is covered by the left hand. Experiments on suspended cadavers have served to prove that a nail passed directly through the palm could not support a body weighing 175 pounds. There is insufficient tissue between the metacarpal bones of the palm to adequately support a nail, and the nail quickly tears through the soft tissues and skin and fails to support the body. A nail, however, placed through the carpal bones and supported by the bones and by the ligaments of the wrist was proved adequate to sustain the weight of a body satisfactorily. The position of the nail still remains a point of minor controversy, although the great weight of evidence indicates that it was placed through the carpal bones, which it separated but did not fracture. The bloodstain on the left wrist is composed of two projecting stains which are separated from one another by approximately a ten-degree angle. This angulation is evidence of the fact that the body while suspended on the cross assumed two different positions in such a way that the blood running from the nail hole in the wrist ran downward from the wrist in two slightly divergent streams. This fact is further supported by examination and measurement of the angles of flow of the blood streams on the forearms. Each of these blood streams on the image extends almost horizontally. If one were able to extend the arms laterally until the blood streams were vertical, it would be found that they are extended in a position approximately sixty-five degrees from the horizontal.

From the positions of the streams of blood both on the wrist and on the forearm, it is obvious that there must have been some other support for the body than the nails in the wrists.

If a person is suspended on a cross even for a brief period of time, by the wrists alone, the pain will be unbearable, and they will die from asphyxiation. However, as soon as a support is provided for the feet, the suspended victim is able to relieve the strain on his wrists and to direct his weight toward his feet. By so doing, he elevates his body to a slight degree by extension of his legs. This change in position is of approximately ten degrees and readily accounts for the divergence in the streams of blood as they pass down the wrists and forearms on the Shroud image. The fact that on the imprint of the hands no thumb is visible is explained by the fact that the nail passing through the bones of the wrist either penetrated or stimulated the median nerve. The motor function of the median nerve is flexion of the thumb, and the flexed thumb over the palm remained in that position after rigor mortis was established and for that reason does not appear on the hand imprint. Some suggestion of the pain suffered by a suspended victim with a nail through or near his median nerve is possible when one realizes that the median nerve is a sensory as well as a motor nerve.

4. THE NAIL MARKS ON THE FEET

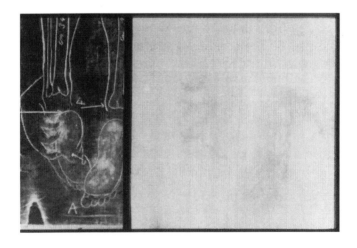

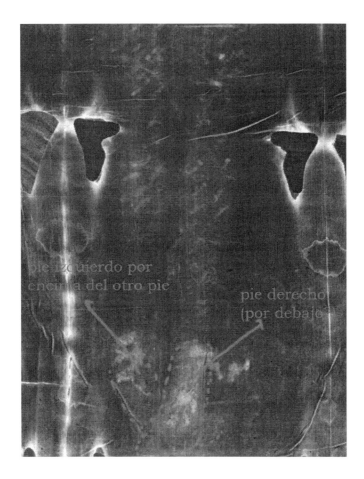

The left foot is shown on top of the right foot

The heel and toe of the right foot are well-
defined, but the left heel is less clear and
elevated above the right heel suggesting that

the left foot was on top of the right instep and a single spike was used to impale the two feet together.

A study of the imprints of the feet is somewhat less complicated than the study of those of the arms and hands. On the Shroud there are two prints representing the marks left by blood-covered feet. One of these, the mark of the right foot, is a nearly complete footprint on which the imprint of the heel and the toes can be seen clearly. In the center of this is a square image surrounded by a pale halo and representing the position of the nail in the foot. The imprint made by the left foot is considerably less clear and does not in any way resemble a footprint. Examination of the calves of the legs on the dorsal view shows that the right calf has left a well-defined imprint on which the marks of the scourge can be well seen. The imprint of the left calf is considerably less distinct, and this, coupled with the fact that the left heel is elevated above the right heel, leads to the conclusion that there is some degree of flexion of the left leg at the knee, and that the development of rigor mortis has left the leg in this position. It appears that the right foot

was directly against the wood of the cross, and
that the left leg was flexed slightly at the knee
and the foot rotated so that the left foot rested
on the instep of the right foot. By this position,
the blood on the soles is accounted for readily.
A single nail was then used to fix both feet in
position. Whether or not there was any other
support for the feet than the wood of the cross
has been a matter of some conjecture, and up
to the present time the point cannot be settled.
The reason for the nailing of the feet was
twofold: the simplest reason was to prevent the
victim from flaying his legs about, but the
second reason was more basic and depended
upon the fact that a victim supported only by
his wrists was unable to survive for more than
a very short time. By having some kind of foot
support, he was able to alternate his position,
resulting in the prolongation of his agony.

This is why the Romans sometimes broke the
legs of crucified victims, removing the foot
support, in order to speed up death.

5. THE WOUND FROM THE CHEST

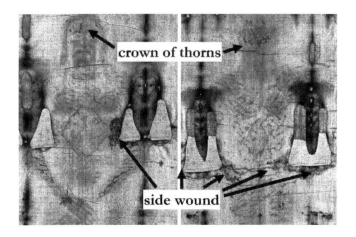

The last of the major wounds on the body of Christ is that in the right side. This wound was made by the lance after death, and although it is partly obliterated by one of several patches on the cloth, its imprint is still clear. This imprint of blood shows the effects of gravity and actual drips, and droplets of blood are clearly seen. There is also evidence of separation of clot from serum. At this point, and also more clearly seen on the dorsal imprint near the lower portion of the back, there is another fluid which has mingled with the blood. In the writing of John, it is stated after the lance pierced the side of Christ, there was an outflow of blood and water. The source of the blood cannot be seriously questioned since it must have come from the heart, and from the position of the blood imprint as well as its structure, it can be assumed that this blood came from the right side of the heart. This chamber was dilated after death and when pierced by the lance, the blood readily flowed from it. A considerable portion of the blood must have dripped onto the ground, but enough was left to form a large stain on the chest and to be later transferred to the Shroud. The source of the water described by John presents more controversy. One possibility is that the fluid represented pericardial fluid. However, the amount of pericardial fluid normally present is in the nature of 20 to 30 cubic centimeters, too small an amount to be seen by the naked eye as it came out of the wound in the side with the blood from the heart.

Another theory is that there was a hydrohemothorax caused by the trauma to the chest by the scourging and increased by the position of the body on the cross prior to death. By gravity the heavier blood could have separated, leaving two layers, and when the lance pierced the side, it released first the blood and then the clear fluid. A combination of the two theories might well explain the situation. An accumulation of fluid in the pleural space without hemorrhage is a logical conclusion as the result of congestive heart failure related to the position of the victim on the cross. It is quite possible that there was a considerable amount of fluid so accumulated, enough that when the lance pierced the side, that fluid would be clearly seen. Then by an actual puncture of the heart there would be an outflow of blood. If the theory of pleural effusion plus puncture of the right side of the heart were sustained, it would be expected that the water would have been visible from the side before the blood and that John's words would have appeared as "water and blood ' rather than "blood and water." As a matter of interest, the words appear in the former sequence in several of the early Greek translations of the New Testament.

When the body was removed from the cross and placed in a horizontal position, there was a second large outflow of blood from the wound in the side. Much of this must have fallen onto the ground, but some stayed on the body and flowed around the right side, leaving a large imprint of clot and serum in the lumbar area. It is in this imprint where the mixture of the blood and the watery fluid is best seen and its presence on the back lends further support to the theory that there was a pleural effusion rather than the water having come from the pericardial sac.

(The thin watery type of substance can best be seen on the dorsal image using ultraviolet photography.)

Dr Robert Bucklin's conclusion was:

"The evidence of a scourged man who was crucified and died from the cardiopulmonary failure typical of crucifixion is clear-cut."

THE SHROUD: THE EVIDENCE

Part 3- The Scientific Examination of 1978

THE SECRET COMMISSION OF 1969

On June 16-17, 1969, a commission appointed by Michele Cardinal Pellegrino of Turin examined the Shroud and concluded that although it was in good condition, measures should be taken to preserve it. Proposals were suggested for further scientific research. Threads from the Shroud were also removed and were found to contain cotton.

In November 1973, Cardinal Pellegrino and the owner of the Shroud at that time, the exiled King Umberto II of Savoy, gave permission for a televised showing of the Shroud. Following this exposition, scientists removed 17 threads from the cloth for analysis.

Their individual findings were published in January 1976 and included Profesor Raes ' discovery of minute cotton fibers mixed in with the linen'. Max Frei had also removed pollen samples with his sticky tape method and found many samples indigenous to plants growing in Palestine and the surrounding area.[26]

These tests paved the way for the 1978 tests undertaken by the STURP team (Shroud of Turin Research Project).

THE 1978 SCIENTIFIC EXAMINATION

It was not until 1978, that the Shroud was allowed to be studied forensically at close range by a team of international scientists in Turin. A large part of that group formed the STURP team, a group of American scientists and researchers who spent over two years preparing a series of tests that would gather a vast amount of Shroud data in a relatively short period of time. They examined it over 5 days round the clock in October 1978, consisting of 120 continuous hours. STURP's main goal was 'to determine the scientific properties of the image on the Shroud of Turin, and what might have caused it'. [27]

THE RESULTS

THE BLOOD ON THE SHROUD

Dr Alan Adler (1931-2000) was a professor of chemistry on the 1978 STURP team, specializing in porphyrins (a type of pigment occurring in animal and plant tissues) and blood chemistry. He spent over 20 years of his life researching and lecturing on the Shroud worldwide as well as contributing to its future conservation.

Adler was invited to join the STURP team by John Heller, who asked him to test the blood on the Shroud of Turin.

Adler replied, 'Being a very well-raised Jew, I said: "What's the Shroud of Turin?' "

John explained to him that they were going to try and prove whether it was the burial cloth of Jesus to which Adler replied, "No, John, that's what we're going to test. Scientists don't prove things, they test things."

Adler turned up the following week fully expecting to see the cloth but was given a sample under a microscope and spent several months creating tests to establish whether it was blood.

Adler was able to verify that the red material on the cloth was indeed blood and not pigment. He tested the blood-derived material left on the cloth and discovered large amounts of a substance called bilirubin that occurs in the blood of a person who has undergone significant physical trauma. The orange color of the bilirubin combined with the brownish color of the haptoglobin-bound-haemoglobin to produce a bright red color that remains red to this day. Adler only discovered small traces of pigment considered to be 'accidentals 'as they accidentally found their way onto the cloth. They were not added by an artist as the body image does not contain any pigment. The reason why pigment was found on the cloth could be explained by several possibilities. Over the centuries, artists made direct copies of the Shroud and may have accidentally or even purposefully left traces of paint as well. There are at least six copies of the Shroud that are known to have been touched to it directly in order to sanctify it. It is very likely traces of pigment were left on the cloth in this way.

If the blood marks were in fact vermillion pigment, this should have shown up when the Shroud was x-rayed as the vermillion would contain mercury. This did not happen. Although iron oxide is found on the Shroud, for this to constitute a pigment, it must contain manganeze, nickel and cobalt. None of these were found and also there was no correlation between the iron concentration and the density of the image. Adler also put forward the proposition as did Ray Rogers, that the water used to douse the fire in 1532, would surely have caused the boundaries of the body image to migrate if it had been painted.

"Our conclusion is that the blood images are derived from the blood of a man who was severely beaten and therefore they got on this cloth by contact and therefore we conclude that this cloth probably enwrapped a human wounded male body, one that had been subjected in fact to some form of severe shock and certainly from the crucifixion marks and the

71

wound marks, it's not hard to find out what the source of the shock would be."[28]

Adler's research on the Shroud lasted until the end of his life.

Dr Alan Adler also reproved a theory by anti-authenticists that blood could have been painted onto the cloth. He explained that blood makes a mess when you try to paint with it as it clots quickly, and substances called inhibitors would have to have been added to the blood which were not available in the 14th century.

Dr Gilbert Lavoie researched Jewish burial customs and found that if the victim died a violent death, blood would not be removed from the body as would normally happen before a Jewish burial.

He conducted tests involving the transfer of blood clots to cloth. The results showed that the cloth must have been on the body within an hour and a half of death or there would have been no transfer due to the process of the clots drying up. The clots begin in liquid form and within 5-10 minutes a biological process takes place turning them into a semi-solid jelly-like state. 20- 40 minutes later, clot retraction occurs meaning the clot gets smaller as it exudes serum. Serum has been found on the cloth around the blood clots and can be seen clearly in the UV photographs taken by Barrie Schwortz, the official documenting photographer on the STURP team. The blood images are revealed to be darker in transmission photographs than in reflection photographs as most of the blood is soaked into the cloth. Adler believed that approximately 25-35% of the material on the surface had migrated from the surface over the years.[29]

Professor Alan Adler 1931-2000

NOTHING ON THE SHROUD CAUSED THE IMAGE

The body image itself is superficial, less than the thickness of a human hair. Dr Eric Jumper, who was instrumental in organizing STURP with Dr John Jackson, stated categorically at the Shroud Symposium of 1986, that the body image is yellow, not red. After probing the threads with a dissecting needle under a microscope, he found no cementing together of the fibrils suggesting that there was nothing on the fibrils. The body image consists of yellow fibrils, not particles, therefore there is nothing on the cloth to cause the body image. The yellow fibrils are a different color from the rest of the cloth due to accelerated ageing. For this to have happened, there needed to have been some kind of catalyst such as intense heat, light or radiation. Jumper or any of other members of the STURP team were not able to identify the catalyst that caused the accelerated decomposition of the cloth as there was no evidence of it remaining, which is a completely normal occurrence. [30]

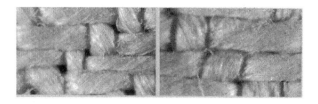

THE IMAGE IS NOT A PHOTOGRAPH

Eric Jumper was an air force scientist at Los Alamos National Scientific Laboratories and worked with Dr John Jackson on the VP-8 Image Analyzer, created specifically for the Space Program.

Designed in the 1970s for evaluating x-rays and for other imaging purposes, the VP-8 Image Analyzer is an analog device that converts image density (lights and darks) into vertical relief (shadows and highlights). In 1976, Jackson and Jumper were part of a group of scientists using a VP-8 to evaluate x-rays when one of the group put a 1931 Enrie photograph of the Shroud of Turin into the device. The results were surprising and unexpected.

The Shroud was seen as a three-dimensional relief of a human form.

When ordinary photographs had been put into the VP-8, the images became a distorted mixture of light and dark areas. This is because the lights and darks of a normal photograph result solely from the amount of light reflected by the subject onto the film, not from the distance the subject was from the film.

However, the Shroud image yielded different properties.

The closer the cloth was to the body (tip of nose, cheekbone, etc.), the darker the image, and the further away (eye sockets, neck, etc.) the fainter the image.

This spatial data encoded into the image actually eliminates photography and painting as the possible mechanism for its creation and allows us to conclude that the image was formed while the cloth was draped over an actual human body.

So, the VP-8 Image Analyzer not only revealed a very important characteristic of the Shroud image, but historically it also provided the actual motivation to form the team that would ultimately go and investigate it.

Dr. John Jackson and Dr. Eric Jumper were two of the researchers present at the test and within a few months of this discovery, had formed the STURP team. Two years later, that same team would perform the first ever, in-depth scientific examination of the Shroud of Turin. [31]

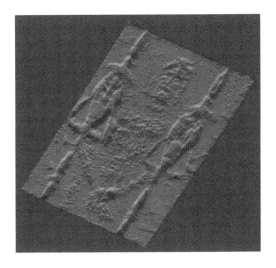

A photograph of the Shroud of Turin under the VP-8 Image Analyzer

Dr John Jackson and Dr Eric Jumper

POST-STURP FINDINGS

POLLEN SHOWS WHERE THE SHROUD HAS BEEN

Prof. Ray Rogers and Dr Max Frei

Dr Max Frei was a botanist and Swiss criminologist who joined the STURP team in 1978. He had come up with the idea of using sticky tape to lift debris off the clothing of crime-scene victims and used this method to remove pollen samples from the Shroud to determine where it had been exposed to the open air.

Frei was one of the first scientists to examine the Shroud on October 8th, 1978, before the American team took over. Shroud historian, Ian Wilson said, "Frei, Columbo-style, took out of his pocket the sort of Scotch tape dispenser that can be purchased in any supermarket and proceeded to press pieces from this into the Shroud with what seemed quite inordinate vigor." [32]

The photographs of the time reveal how hard Frei was pushing into the cloth by how high it was pulled up with the sticky tape as it was removed.

Frei was about to apply the sticky tape to the face, the most iconic part of the cloth, when John Jackson stepped in and pulled him away at the last moment. They almost came to blows and after a few minutes of heated discussion, it was decided that nobody was to put sticky tape on the face.

Frei was severely criticized in some quarters for his aggressive sticky tape methods compared to the specialized method of the STURP team in applying a minimum, exact, and uniform pressure with the high-grade Mylar tape. [33]

However, Frei's method worked. The STURP sticky tape picked up only one pollen sample and the special Mylar tape proved less than satisfactory for microscopic work. Frei's tape picked up hundreds of deep-seated pollen spores along with other particles that have been examined extensively by many researchers. Among the particles collected on the tape were dust, pollen, plant and insect parts, blood from the blood stains on the Shroud, and loose fibrils of the fabric.

However, it remains to be seen if the gummy residue from the cheap sticky tape may have caused some long-term damage to cloth.

Many doubted Frei's findings, with some accusing him of fraud which was proven to be unfounded. In 1982, the archaeologist Paul C. Maloney contacted Frei to ask why, in his opinion, he had found so many pollen grains while STURP scientists had found only one pollen grain in their samples. The Swiss scientist answered Maloney quite matter-of-factly that the difference was due to the different pressure carried in applying the sticky tape on the Shroud.

Once the pollen was located, more information was available concerning the Shroud's whereabouts in the past. There were those who believed the pollen could have travelled from great distances negating the geographical evidence it provided but Frei disagreed:

"90% of the pollen production of a given plant is deposited within 100 meters. A propagation to a distance of tens of kilometers is still considered normal, while exceptionally strong winds in times of drought (sirocco) are responsible for rare extremely far transports of hundreds or thousands of kilometers. (...) In the case of the Shroud the represented plants bloom in different seasons and live in well-defined, and different from each other, ecological conditions. Their pollen is not especially suited to very far transports.

Therefore, the heterogeneity and the amount of pollen cannot be explained on the basis of random contamination".[34]

Frei identified pollen spores of 58 different plants, many that originate only in and around Jerusalem and areas of the Middle East that include the ancient cities of Constantinople and Edessa.

Frei's death in 1983 meant his book remained unfinished and was sadly, never published.

FLOWER IMAGES ON THE CLOTH HELP IDENTIFY WHEN THE IMAGE FORMED

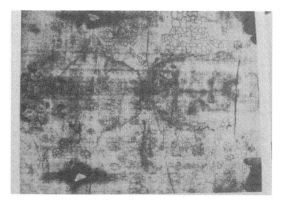

The flower image on the Shroud is located between the image on the left which Scheuermann produced by corona discharge and the drawing on the right of a Chrysanthemum coronarium from Flora Palaestina. The image on the Shroud resembles that of a slightly wilted flower about 24–36 hours after having been picked. Drawing

Also in 1983, German physicist Dr Oswald Scheuermann noticed flower images on photographs of the Shroud and communicated his discovery to Dr Alan Whanger, a Duke University Professor of Psychiatry, with whom he had been corresponding about experiments with high-voltage corona discharges to produce Shroud-like images on linen.[35]

Although Frei was looking for pollen that had attached itself to the Shroud in air-born fashion, pollen would also have come from the flowers buried with the body. The abundance of flower images around the head coincides with the large amount of pollen found there and an imprint of a chrysanthemum can still be seen to the left of the head. [36]

Whanger identified images of 28 different flowers which due to the degree of wilting and dehydration observed, would have been picked 24-36 hours before their images were imprinted on the Shroud. This reinforces the evidence that the body image was imprinted 24-40 hours after death, indicated by the presence of rigor mortis seen on the body image.

Twenty of the flower images seen on the Shroud were found to grow in Jerusalem with the other eight being found 15 miles within Jerusalem.

Most of the flowers were clustered around the head and chest of the man on the Shroud which was the Jewish burial custom in the time of Jesus.

The flowers can be seen more clearly in the photographs of Giuseppe Enrie, taken in 1931, indicating that the background cloth has grown more yellow since then, making these images harder to identify.

The Justinian coin and the Pantocrator image, believed to be direct copies of the Shroud, show subtle images of flowers around the head, indicating also that the imprints were a lot clearer to the naked eye in the 7th century. Coins, being numismatic icons, would mean a copier would attempt to reproduce the original image as closely as possible.[37]

Dr Whanger (1930-2017) and his wife, Mary visited Jerusalem in 1995 and met with Israeli botanist Dr. Avinoam Danin (1939-2015), of Jerusalem's Hebrew University and Dr. Uri Baruch, a palynologist (science of pollen and spores) and authority on Israeli antiquities.

Danin studied the plant images and Baruch analyzed the pollen grains found by Max Frei.[38]

They confirmed his findings and verified that 27 of the identified plants are in bloom in Israel in the vicinity of Jerusalem in March and April, a period consistent with the time of the Passover and the Crucifixion.

Furthermore, half of the floral images and pollen grains from the plants are found only in the Middle East or other similar areas but never in Europe, the favored location of the forgery of the Shroud.[39]

The scientists 'analyses positively identified many grains of pollen from a plant called 'Gundelia tournefortii 'which has large thorns and blooms in Israel between March and May.

Most of the grains of pollen from that plant have been recovered near the man's shoulder.

It has been suggested that the Crown of Thorns may have been made from Gundelia tournefortii.

The pollen of Gundelia tournefortii and that of Zygophyllum dumosum are the most significant types to have been found on the Shroud and are necessary for locating its origin.

Danin stated "As Zygophyllum dumosum grows only in Israel, Jordan and Sinai, its appearance helps to definitely limit the Shroud's place of origin."[40]

(In 1997, Dr. Danin advised: "Both species (Zygophyllum dumosum and Gundelia tournefortii) are necessary for locating the origin of the Shroud."

Dr Whanger also developed a technique called, 'Polarised Image Overlay 'whereby he claimed to find many points of congruence between the Christ Pantocrator icon (c 550AD) from St Catherine's Monastery in Mount Sinai and the Shroud. This image was found to have

11 of the 15 Vignon markings found on the Shroud. Many Vignon markings have been identified in depictions of Christ from the 6th century onwards raising the question: Was the Shroud directly copied from this time onwards and used as a model of how Christ appeared?

LINKS WITH THE SUDARIUM OF OVIEDO

Interestingly the Sudarium of Ovideo has also been analyzed for pollen and shares two of the same pollen types found on the Shroud. The Sudarium ('facecloth 'in Latin) is believed to have been wrapped around the head of Jesus after his death on the cross in order to absorb the blood on his face.

According to Jewish tradition, this would then have been removed and buried with him in the tomb as the lifeblood is considered sacred.

Simon Peter who was following now came up, went right into the tomb, saw the linen cloths on the ground, and also the cloth that had been over his head; this was not with the linen cloths but rolled up in a place by itself. Then the other disciple who had reached the tomb first also went in; he saw and he believed. Till this moment they had failed to understand the teaching of scripture, that he must rise from the dead.

The Gospel of John 20: v 6-9 (The Jerusalem Bible)

However, pollen on the Sudarium was found from different areas to the Shroud indicating a different route taken from Palestine in 614 AD and then through North Africa to Spain. The pollen on the facecloth reveals it has been in the open air in Africa at some time but there is no evidence of it being in Constantinople or Anatolia as with the Shroud. The Shroud and the Sudarium share the same blood type AB, the rarest blood type and the formation of the blood stains on the Sudarium coincides with the blood stains on the face of the Shroud.

The Sudarium is found in the cathedral of Oviedo in Spain, where it is displayed to the public three times a year on Good Friday, the Feast of the Triumph of the Cross (14 September) and its octave (21 September). Radiocarbon testing dated it to c700 AD, a much older result than the carbon dates given for the Shroud and raising yet another debate as to its authenticity.[41]

UNKNOWN OBJECTS ON THE SHROUD

1. COINS ON EYES?

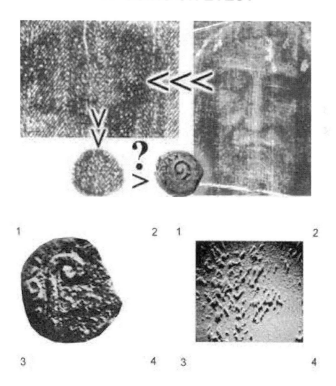

The VP-8 image analyzer that revealed the Shroud contained distance information and began the formation of the STURP team, also pointed to the presence of some objects around and on the face. There was evidence of an object wrapped around the head, considered by many to be a chin bandage. This would have been used to prevent the mouth from falling open in rigor mortis. There was also the appearance of circular objects on the eyes as well as an object resting on the neck. Conforming to ancient Jewish burial custom, pottery fragments or coins were sometimes placed over the eyes of the deceased.

Jumper, Stevenson, and Jackson submitted an article to the coin magazine, The Numismatist, (July 1978) proposing the theory that the three-dimensional images of objects over the eyes on the man of the Shroud of Turin might be coins. These images of the two objects are nearly circular and each about the same size, between 1-5 mm thick, with an average diameter of about 14 mm. They suggested that if they were in fact coins, it could be a way of dating the Shroud image. Ian Wilson believed a lepton coin featuring Pontius Pilate was an especially close match for the size of the objects.

In 1979, Fr. Francis Filas (1915-85), Professor of Theology at Loyola University of Chicago, was examining an enlargement of the Shroud's face image on an Enrie 1931 sepia print and noticed a design over the right eye. [42]

Filas showed the print to Michael Marx, a Chicago coin expert, who examined the right eye with a magnifier and confirmed the presence of four Greek capital letters in a curve, which appeared to be "ECAI", later realizing that the "E" was actually a "U". Filas theorised that the letters "UCAI" were part of the inscription "TIBEPIOUKAICAPOC" ("Of Tiberius Caesar") or of the abbreviation "TIOUKAICAPOC" ("Of Caesar") with the "C" being an alternative spelling of "K". The letters curved around a Roman **astrologer's staff called a lituus**, a motif used on Roman coins minted by Pontius Pilate between AD 29-32.

Filas had in his possession a Pontius Pilate lepton coin with the rare variant "UCAI" misspelling that had previously not been known to have existed. In the next two years Filas was shown two other Pontius leptons with the "K" in

"KAICAPOC" misspelled "C". This coin can be specifically dated to 29 AD.

Dr Whanger was also able to identify the letters "LIH" on a photograph of the obverse side of Filas' coin. The letters "LIH" stand for the sixteenth year of the reign of Tiberius Caesar, which is AD 29. This AD 29 date of Filas' coin was independently confirmed by William Pettit, Research Specialist for the Standard Catalog of World Coins.[43] [44]

However, these objects identified on the eyes of the image have never been scientifically verified as coins and may be seen as possibilities that have not yet been proven beyond reasonable doubt.

2. UNKNOWN OBJECT ON NECK

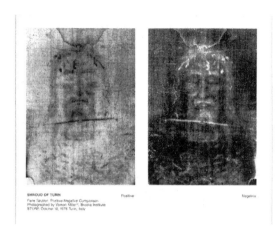

SHROUD OF TURIN
Face Sculptin Positive-Negative Comparison
Photographed by Vernon Miller", Brooks Institute
STURP, October 10, 1978 Turin, Italy   Positive   Negative

Dr Petrus Soons used the 3D data provided by
the VP-8 image analyzer to produce
holographic images of the Shroud. In 2005,

with a team of experts, he produced the first hologram of the face on the Shroud and life-size holograms of the front and the back of the body soon followed. In May of 2010 the presence of this solid object was scientifically confirmed by research done by Pete Schumacher with the VP-8 Analyzer.

Dr Petrus Soons identified three Hebrew letters on the surface of this object on the neck of the man on the Shroud, that he recognized thanks to his knowledge of calligraphy. He showed the letters to experts in Hebrew in Jerusalem, Rome and the Oriental Institute in Oxford to ask for the meaning of these letters, or if they formed a known word. [45]

Most experts did not want to give a definitive answer, due to the lack of detail available but Soons was shown the dictionary of Ernest Klein, "A Comprehensive Etymological Dictionary of the Hebrew Language for Readers of English" and told that these letters formed the word TS'ON. According to this dictionary the meaning of the word TS'ON is:

"small cattle, sheep and goats". However, in Exodus 12:21, TS'ON is translated differently.

When the Israelites are ordered by God to prepare a lamb for sacrifice and after the sacrifice put the blood on the doorposts, the word that is used for lamb is SEH (Exodus 12:3) and that is correct. However, in Exodus 12:21 it says: "Then Moses summoned all the elders of Israel and said to them, "Go at once and select the animals for your families and slaughter the Passover lamb". The word that is used in the Bible is TS'ON and this is the ONLY TIME in the whole of the Bible that the word TS'ON is used as lamb, and it is specifically translated as such for this occasion. [46]

In the Bible, Jesus Christ is the Passover lamb, dying at the same moment on Good Friday, when in the Temple the annual sacrifice of the lambs took place for the forgiveness of sins.

A SUMMARY OF STURP'S CONCLUSIONS

'After years of exhaustive study and evaluation of the data, STURP issued its Final Report in 1981. The following official summary of their conclusions was distributed at the press conference held after their final meeting in October 1981, *'Barrie Schwortz (Official Documenting Photographer):*

No pigments, paints, dyes or stains have been found on the fibrils. X-ray, fluorescence and microchemistry on the fibrils preclude the possibility of paint being used as a method for creating the image. Ultraviolet and infrared evaluation confirm these studies. Computer image enhancement and analysis by a device known as a VP-8 image analyzer show that the image has unique, three-dimensional information encoded in it. Microchemical evaluation has indicated no evidence of any spices, oils, or any biochemicals known to be produced by the body in life or in death. It is clear that there has been a direct contact of the Shroud with a body, which explains certain features such as scourge marks, as well as the blood. However, while this type of contact might explain some of the features of the torso, it is totally incapable of explaining the image of the face with the high resolution that has been amply demonstrated by photography.

The basic problem from a scientific point of view is that some explanations which might be tenable from a chemical point of view, are precluded by physics. Contrariwise, certain physical explanations which may be attractive are completely precluded by the chemistry. For an adequate explanation for the image of the Shroud, one must have an explanation which is scientifically sound, from a physical, chemical, biological and medical viewpoint. At the present, this type of solution does not appear to be obtainable by the best efforts of the members of the Shroud Team. Furthermore, experiments in physics and chemistry with old linen have failed to reproduce adequately the phenomenon presented by the Shroud of Turin. The scientific consensus is that the image was produced by something which resulted in oxidation, dehydration and conjugation of the polysaccharide structure of the microfibrils of the linen itself. Such changes can be duplicated in the laboratory by certain chemical and physical processes. A similar type of change in linen can be obtained by sulfuric acid or heat. However, there are no chemical or physical methods known which can account for the totality of the image, nor can any combination of physical, chemical, biological or medical circumstances explain the image adequately.

Thus, the answer to the question of how the image was produced or what produced the image remains, now, as it has in the past, a mystery.

We can conclude for now that the Shroud image is that of a real human form of a scourged, crucified man. It is not the product of an artist. The blood stains are composed of hemoglobin and also give a positive test for serum albumin. The image is an ongoing mystery and until further chemical studies are made, perhaps by this group of scientists, or perhaps by some scientists in the future, the problem remains unsolved.[47]

Part 4- The Shroud Declared a Fake

Although scientific evidence pointed to the Shroud being genuine, the carbon-14 dating results of 1988 refuted this.

Interestingly, after preliminary tests were undertaken on the sample threads of the Shroud in 1973, Dr Codegone published a dissertation on the inadvisability of performing carbon-14 tests on the Shroud believing that tests would not produce a reliable result. Professor Lorenzi also agreed that radiological tests would be unlikely to produce meaningful results.[48]

It is arguable that contaminants produced over the centuries from the Shroud's encounters with fire and water could have skewed the results.

However, it cannot be argued that the samples taken for carbon dating should have been taken from different areas of the cloth to produce a credible result. In 1984, the STURP team advised in writing that three samples from three different areas of the cloth should be taken for testing as did others before the test took place. Despite this, samples were taken from one area only, adjacent to the Raes sample area, which was near a corner of the Shroud and would consequently have been handled a great deal when displayed. It was later realized to have been an area that had been repaired perhaps due to this reason or perhaps parts of the cloth had been taken as relics.[49]

On studying the radiographs of the Shroud made in 1978, details of the seams and threads can be seen. It appears that the side seam was put in as a tuck, and that near the two missing corners there are variations in weave patterns and in thread densities which suggest that these two areas had been damaged and then repaired in some way. Examination of the site of the C-14 single sample indicates that at least part of the sample was taken from one of these repaired or altered areas.

In 1988, laboratories in Oxford, Zurich and Tucson, Arizona were chosen to carbon date samples of the Shroud to determine its true age. Originally, two methods were to be used by seven laboratories, but this idea was discarded apparently due to more material being needed. The decision was heavily criticized as was the decision to take samples from only one area of the cloth. This is significant because, if the chosen portion was in any way not representative of the remainder of the Shroud, the results would only be applicable to that portion of the cloth... which is exactly what happened.

After a heated argument, Riggi and Gonella, the Turin scientists, made the decision, (on the spot), of removing samples from the left-hand corner of the cloth, where material had been cut away previously. These samples were then given to the laboratories. On October 13, 1988, at a press conference at the British Museum, the radiocarbon dates for the Shroud were written on a blackboard as '1260-1390!'. Hall,

Tite and Hedges of the Oxford radiocarbon dating lab declared the Shroud a medieval fake, a conclusion which is still believed by many today despite evidence to the contrary that has since emerged. Professor Hall likened believers to 'flat-earthers 'and no other side was presented.

However, Joseph Marino, a former Benedictine monk, and his late wife, Sue Benford, had their doubts. They had seen the ultraviolet photographs of the Shroud and noted that the area where the samples had been taken appeared as green, indicating a different chemical composition to the rest of the Shroud. They believed the cloth had been rewoven in that area.

Benford said, "When you do this type of reweaving, you're not just stitching two pieces of material together which would give you all of one and all of the other. The ends are unraveled in the main cloth and in the patch and they are spliced together, and the threads are connected and interwoven so that you have old and new on both sides of the equation."

Barrie Schwortz, the official photographer from the STURP team met the couple and said, "I was skeptical and listening to this, but they had taken photographs that were available of the samples taken for carbon dating and had submitted these to textile experts who didn't know they were looking at a photograph from the Shroud. Each of these textile experts, independent of each other, said, 'You know, this looks rewoven'. "

Bedford and Marino presented a paper at the Sindone 2000 World Congress in Orvieto, Italy, hypothesizing that the reason the 1988 C-14 dating of the Shroud resulted in a date range of AD 1260-1390 for the cloth was because a sixteenth-century repair in the sample area had resulted in an average of dates between the 1st and 16th century.

When this theory was suggested to Ray Rodgers of the STURP team (Shroud of Turin Research Project), he hit the roof. He had little patience with amateur scientists and when Barrie Schwortz suggested he test it out, he readily agreed. Rogers had tendrils from the surface of the Shroud and samples from 1973 from the corner adjacent to the area taken for carbon dating. However, when he called Schwortz back, his mood had changed to shock after finding cotton interwoven in the samples. He was eventually able to examine thread from part of the samples retained by the laboratories, which split in two to reveal cotton and linen. Not only this, but Rogers knew from his own tests in 1978 that the Shroud was free of dye and artificial pigments, but he found dye on the surviving threads of the carbon dating samples. As linen is very difficult to dye, cotton is used and dyed to match the linen.

Rogers 'findings were published in 2005 in the prestigious, peer-reviewed journal, Thermochimica Acta and since then, other scientists have independently verified Ray Rogers 'conclusion that the carbon dating tests did not reveal the Shroud's true age. No doubt was cast on the science of carbon dating but that the sample taken was contaminated.

Rogers stated, "I'm coming to the conclusion that it has a very good chance of being the piece of cloth that was used to bury the historic Jesus."[50]

More evidence was found on the Shroud in July 2017, indicating that the man on the cloth had been tortured. Very small particles attached to its linen fibers, were identified as containing high levels of the substances, creatinine and ferritin, often found in patients who have suffered multiple traumas. Correlating with previous evidence, this points to a violent death for the man wrapped in the Turin Shroud.[51]

Science once dismissed the Shroud as fake, but science can also deepen our faith and understanding of this mysterious cloth that refuses to be labelled. One thing is certain, the Shroud raises more questions than it answers and how the imprint was formed, remains a mystery

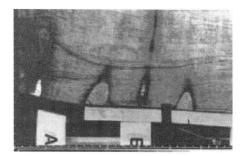

UV Fluorescence photograph of the Shroud. The dark green colour in the bottom left indicates the presence of cotton. This is the area the Raes sample was taken from, and the samples sent to different laboratories which were carbon dated.

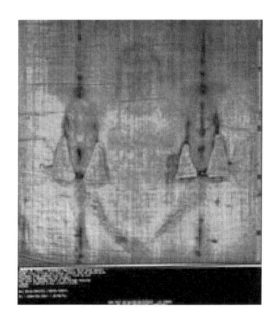

FOOTNOTE

In 1982, a single piece of thread was believed to have been taken from the Shroud and sent surreptitiously to a West Coast Laboratory to be carbon dated. This was unofficial and believed to have been a 'dry-run 'for the carbon dating tests of 1988. The results proved inconclusive as one end of the thread was allegedly dated to 200 AD, while the other end resulted in a date of ca. 1000/1200 AD.

William Meacham, an archaeologist and author wrote: "[John] Heller took me back to the train station that evening [in 1984], and as we sat waiting for my train back to New York City, he told me in strictest confidence about a secret C-14 run that had already been made on a thread from the Shroud. He said it had been done by the Livermore Laboratory in California, and the thread was cut into two segments. One end dated ca. 200 AD., and the other ca. 1000 A.D. He also said that starch had been identified on the thread. He did not know what margin of error there was on the dates, and thought it would be quite wide, as the test was only intended to give a rough idea of what an eventual C-14 date would look like. As it turned out, it gave conflicting indications. (This test in California was later confirmed to me by [Alan] Adler, who said that he was in fact the one who had arranged it, despite C-14 dating being specifically forbidden in STURP's agreement with the Turin Archdiocese.)" [52]

If the thread in question was taken from the same area near the Rae's corner where the carbon dating samples were taken from, there is a good chance they were testing a contaminated piece of material. This would fit with the Benford-Marino-Rogers 'research that the thread was a spliced sample of linen and cotton. It is then quite conceivable that the carbon dating was correct and produced a wide variation in dates because two types of material were tested.

Heller and Adler discussed the test in an interview with Case in 1994. Heller was seriously ill in a wheelchair at the time and died the following year. It seems unlikely under the circumstances that he would confirm the test took place if it had not. Mark Antonacci also writes, "Several STURP scientists have also confirmed these datings [from the 1982 test] to me and other researchers after this information was first published."[53]

Did the 1982 test take place? Probably. But since it was not an official, recorded test, it cannot be used as evidence. It does however underscore the inconsistencies of the cloth in the area tested in 1988.

THE SHROUD: THE EVIDENCE

Part 5- Personal experience

A few years before this discovery, I had seen the blood on the Shroud at close range during an exposition in 2015. Although it had only been on display 5 years earlier, Pope Francis had given his permission for another showing in the Year of Mercy. I had always wanted to see it and yet now I wondered if it would mean anything to me as doubt and scepticism had crept into my mind. Once, I had believed it to be Christ's burial cloth without question from the feeling that it touched my soul; but as I moved away from my faith, the memory of this feeling left my mind, and I forgot his face… temporarily. Now, my memory was stirred. I booked my flight.

Before I left for Turin, I discovered that Barrie Schwortz would be in Turin during this time too and I contacted him for an interview. It was while I was researching his background as a member of the STURP team (Shroud of Turin

Research Project) which examined the Shroud over 5 days in 1978, that I realized the irony: scientific evidence was, in fact, pointing to its authenticity.

In Turin, Barrie generously gave me over 3 hours of his time (although he has often said, "It's easy to get me to start talking but harder to get me to stop!")

Schwortz was working as a photographer specializing in scientific, medical and technical issues when he was asked to join the STURP team. He originally refused mainly because he was skeptical and uncomfortable with the subject matter. However, the Shroud's scientific properties piqued his curiosity and he joined yet still tried to quit twice again.

Barrie talked about his doubts to Don Lynn, a fellow member of the STURP team and an imaging expert from NASA's jet propulsion laboratory. The conversation went something like this:

"Don, what's a nice Jewish boy like me doing on this team?"

"Have you forgotten that the man in question was a Jew?"

"No Don, that's probably the only thing I know about Jesus that he was a Jew."

"So you don't think that God would want one of his chosen people on our team?"

"No Don, I never thought that."

"Barrie, go to Turin, do the best job you can do, God doesn't tell us in advance what the plan is but one day you'll know."

On these words, Barrie stayed on the team.

The tests went on to prove that the Shroud was not a painting, not a scorch mark and not a photograph but could only confirm what it was not. After that, it took another 18 years before Schwortz was finally convinced of its authenticity.

His reservations came from the bright red blood on the cloth which should have turned brown after a few hours but was still red despite its claim to being almost 2,000 years old. Alan Adler, a expert in blood chemistry, later explained to Schwortz, that he had found a high content of bilirubin in the blood on the cloth. Bilirubin breaks down red blood cells to release hemoglobin, causing blood stains to always remain red.

Barrie said, 'When a man is beaten and has had no water, he can go into shock and the liver starts pumping out bilirubin. It makes the blood stay red forever. It was the last piece of the puzzle for me. I had nothing left to complain about. Sometimes I wonder why I hadn't asked Alan Adler that question 17 years before, but I guess I wasn't ready for the answer back then.'

I marveled then and now at science once dismissing the Shroud as a medieval forgery, and yet continuing to produce evidence that points in the opposite direction to the bafflement and indignation of many sceptics.

I said a fond goodbye to Barrie and went to see the Shroud for myself.

After following many winding paths, I finally
found myself in a small, tented room where a
film was shown before entering the cathedral.
The room darkened and the crowd watched in
silent wonder as close-ups of the main wounds
were labelled in different languages. As the
lights went up, a sense of awe hung in the air
and a more profound awareness that what we
were about to see was extremely special.

It was while striding along the last pathway, I
had my own strange encounter which began as
a feeling of heaviness in my head. It felt like a
mysterious and ancient love. How does anyone
describe holiness?

It grew stronger as I approached, like
something I had felt before around certain
relics. Some may understand this, and others
may not but there is a timelessness as when
receiving Holy Communion. This strange sense
of a presence that occupied my being, grew,
refusing to be ignored as did my excitement as
I gained some small sense of what I was about
to see and yet could not grasp its magnitude.

We were ushered through to the dark
cathedral. As I stood in line, suddenly and

without warning, the face on the Shroud revealed itself through a gap in the curtain in front of me. In that quick moment, I felt a pleasant shock seeing it illuminated and so clearly defined above the altar, ancient and yet timeless; timeless because there was nothing between me and this mysterious imprint. Was it seen by the disciples and Mary? Who knows but it felt real as did the intimacy in this private moment as though Jesus were right in front of me, so familiar, so holy and so full of love.

The five minutes in front of the Turin Shroud were not enough. I tried to drink in everything I saw, then my time was up, and we were moved through the darkness and out of the cathedral. One last look behind, made possible by knowing I would be back, and I was out into the hot sunny day. I sat in the shade and felt moved to tears. Something had overwhelmed me, and I felt a strong love within me for him.

After a time, we may forget a spiritual experience or tell ourselves it was purely a personal response and dismiss it. Maybe this is just us conforming to the world for a while until Jesus wakes us up again.

May we learn to trust in him, over the world.

THE SHROUD: THE EVIDENCE

CONTEMPLATIONS ON THE SHROUD

The reading from Isaiah (53:3) comes to mind...

(He was) a thing despised and rejected by men,

a man of sorrows, and familiar with suffering.

a man to make people screen their faces;

he was despised, and we took no account of him.

1. Staying with his Suffering

Can we look at the beaten and bruised, scourged and wounded body of the man on the Shroud and stay with the feeling that arises within?

The pain that comes from having some small understanding of how much suffering he endured, which is true compassion, is compounded by the humility and dignity of the man believers know to be Jesus Christ.

No other man could bear such intense and overwhelming suffering on all levels- mental, emotional, physical and spiritual- and this man, instead of showing the excruciating strain on his face of a horrific death, seems to reach out to us with peace, dignity and love.

Do any non-believers consider the ethereal beauty of the face on the cloth? It is never mentioned. They either refuse to see it or their eyes are blinded to his holiness. Even if definitive proof of the Resurrection was found through the formation of the image, the more ardent anti-authenticists would find an argument against the evidence. Why? It is too incredible, and they will not concede to the idea of a creator god. They cannot and will not submit their will and surrender their being to their maker as perhaps it may seem they are losing control rather than gaining their freedom and being loved by love itself. We as followers of Christ, on the other hand, must always choose compassion over anger and persist in the truth.

So do not turn away from his suffering.

The Blessed Virgin Mary, St John, St Mary Magdalene and others who loved him, stayed at the foot of the Cross. How painful must that have been, but they remained there because of their great love for him. How could they leave him? Compassion is to be with someone in their suffering and they stood with him until the end.

Although it can be painful to look at his suffering, it is an act of love towards Jesus to stay with him and not turn away. He went through the Passion out of love for us and out of love and obedience to the Father, he gave his life willingly. Can we not spend some time contemplating this act of love which can only bring us closer to him?

We can deepen our love and faith in Jesus Christ by contemplating his face and his wounds, allowing the Passion to penetrate our souls more deeply.

Now if we believe, we believe and that goes
without question, but by actually looking at the
wounds and the suffering shown on the
Shroud, we are transported to a deeper love of
Jesus within the depths of our soul where it
has the possibility to heal.

Deeply pondering the Resurrection, can bring a
greater depth and love to our faith and joy of
life.

He has gained victory over death, and he lives
within us therefore his victory belongs to us.

Let us begin to live more in this eternal victory.
The joy that overflows from this will bring a
deep happiness and a steady peace to both
ourselves and others in this journey called life.

Make the time on a regular basis to meditate
on the Shroud image. It is easy to obtain a
copy of the Holy Face. The more you lose
yourself in it, the more you will experience the
beauty, the nobility and the humility in his
presence. He seems to be sending out a great
love. How is this possible after having died in
the way he did? After hours of intense physical
pain, being beaten, scourged and then

crucified alongside the mental torture of being rejected, mocked and betrayed, there is a sense of calmness that radiates peace and love. Is this Jesus in the moment of the Resurrection? His beaten, dead body in the moment of life suffusing through it?

There is no way of knowing but through the eyes of faith we can see and believe.

2. Holy Moments

Who was the person who sowed the seeds out of which came the flax for our Lord's burial cloth? Did they pray as they did their work? How could they have known how special that moment was; what it would lead to? And what of the person who picked the flax that was spun to make the linen cloth. Perhaps for them, it was another ordinary day but how wrong this would be. Was the person who wove the cloth thinking of other mundane things that they needed to do afterwards or were they in silent prayer? Was there a sense of something special, even for just one moment and did this pass them by as other unimportant things crowded this feeling out, stopping them from seeing the Lord in everything, always.

How could they have known on that day they played a part in making the burial cloth of the Son of God... that it was the most significant moment of their life. How can we know when a moment carries such weight of meaning? Unless we have an acute sense of intuition, we cannot fully know, therefore we should live in the goodness of every moment, knowing that each moment is and will lead to something beautiful and holy and may we respect that. Every moment can be a holy moment if we rest in it instead of being distracted by trivial thoughts. This requires practice but we can learn to experience life fully and instead of rejecting or desiring certain experiences, understand that everything comes from God and be curious as to what he is bringing us.

To live with acceptance and joy of the will of God, can only bring greater peace and a deep happiness that nothing can take away.

Living for God is true happiness.

3. The Blood of Love

We are told that the cloth for the Shroud came from Joseph of Arimathea, a rich man who could afford the finest linen. Nobody can know its true origins for certain, but we know its purpose; to cover the Lord and soak up his Precious Blood and bear witness to the Crucifixion and Resurrection.

As his beaten body was lowered onto the cloth, the white linen, became red, stained with his Precious Blood. In any other case, this would make it an object of revulsion, but in this case and only this case, it became priceless and precious beyond all measure.

Out of love for him, the ones left at the foot of the Cross put aloes, myrrh and flowers around his bloodied body. They were not repulsed by his appearance but loved him all the more. How long did they look before finally having to lower the Shroud over the body for the last time? How difficult was that moment? As the white linen descended over his torso, his Precious Blood would have instantly penetrated the cloth. The violence done to him was inescapable. But his Blood was beautiful from the sacrifice made for us out of love. They saw love while others turned away in disgust.

Now covered from head to toe in the white and blood-stained linen, how hard was it to leave their beloved master and dear friend there, lying alone in the tomb? As far as they knew, it was the last time. How difficult to leave him! Perhaps Mary had knowledge and faith that he would return but that could not have provided any relief from her sorrow. Although she was to return with the women to anoint his body, how her heart must have felt broken.

They gazed upon the linen cloth covering his body yet revealing his Blood that redeemed us and blessed be God, we still have that same linen cloth today.

PRAYER FOR THE SHROUD

We pray that the Shroud will always be protected and conserved. May it lead many to the belief that Jesus was truly man and truly Son of God.

We pray also that more mysteries will be revealed that exist on the cloth but are not yet known. May more evidence arise that points to the authenticity of the cloth. May it be a steppingstone for many towards faith in Christ and may it deepen the faith of those who already believe.

We ask this in the name of Our Lord Jesus Christ, the Son of the Living God who is beyond all human understanding.

Blessed be God forever,

Amen

THE SHROUD: THE EVIDENCE

Photographs of Shroud Exhibitions

Engraving of the Shroud- 1613

The cathedral during the 1898 exhibition

Outside the cathedral- 1933

1933 exhibition of the Shroud

1978 exhibition of the Shroud

Footnotes

[1] 1986 talk-The Shroud Symposium.

https://www.youtube.com/watch?v=yuF1MPIA9-w&t=1539s

[2] The Shroud-Ian Wilson (p191)

[3] The Shroud-Ian Wilson (p190)

[4] Codex Vossianus Latinus, Q69, and Vatican Library, Codex 5696, fol.35, which was published in Pietro Savio, Ricerche storiche sulla Santa Sindone Turin 1957

[5] The Image of Edessa, Brill, Leiden & Boston, 2009- Mark Guscin

[6] The Shroud-Ian Wilson- p177

[7] The Shroud- Ian Wilson- p183

[8] The Shroud- Ian Wilson- p209-212

[9]
https://www.academia.edu/913214/Relics_of_the_Pharos_Chapel _A_View_from_the_Latin_West

[10] https://en.wikipedia.org/wiki/Fourth_Crusade

[11] The Shroud- Ian Wilson- p246-248

[12] The Shroud- Ian Wilson- p270

[13] The Shroud- Ian Wilson-p266

[14] The Shroud- Ian Wilson-p392

[15] Translation by Mark Guscin, author of 'The Oviedo Cloth '

(1998, Lutterworth Press)

https://www.shroud.com/pdfs/guscin3.pdf

[16] https://www.shroud.com/history.htm

[17] A.Tonelli- La fotografia ha deciso, Rivista dei Giovani, Torino
(November 1929)

[18] L.Fossati- Un oscuro promotore della ripresa fotografica della
Sacra Sindone nel 1898: il salesiano Don Natale Noguier de
Malijay,

Collegamento pro Sindone, July/August 1988 pp.8-42 The name of
Pia's assistant was Carlino

http://www.acheiropoietos.info/proceedings/FalcinelliPiaWeb.pdf

[19] de Wesselow, 2012, pp.18-19

[20] http://theshroudofturin.blogspot.com/2016/12/negative-19-man-
on-shroud-evidence-is.html#paraGPB

[21] http://theshroudofturin.blogspot.com/2016/12/negative-19-man-
on-shroud-evidence-is.html

[22] The Shroud of Turin: A Case for Authenticity-By Rev. Fr. Vittorio Guerrera- Ch5

[23] http://shroud3d.com/making-of-the-holograms/enrie-photographs

[24] http://crc-internet.org/our-doctrine/catholic-counter-reformation/holy-shroud-turin/1-precious-blood-jesus/

[25] https://www.shroud.com/bucklin2.htm

[26] The Shroud of Turin: A Case for Authenticity-By Rev. Fr. Vittorio Guerrera- Ch5

[27] https://www.shroud.com/78exam.htm

[28] https://www.youtube.com/watch?v=T3ZEkEjA4Uw

[29] https://www.youtube.com/watch?v=gzDTMmUvGpc

[30] https://www.youtube.com/watch?v=yuF1MPIA9-w&t=913s

[31] https://www.shroud.com/78strp10.htm

[32] http://www.theholyshroud.net/Pollens.htm

[33] http://www.theholyshroud.net/Pollens.htm

35https://www.researchgate.net/publication/291332538_The_question_of_pollen_grains_on_the_Shroud_of_Turin_and_the_Sudarium_of_Oviedo

THE SHROUD: THE EVIDENCE

[35] http://theshroudofturin.blogspot.co.uk/2013/04/the-shroud-of-turin-26-other-marks-4.html

[36] https://www.shroud.com/danin2.htm

[37] https://www.shroud.com/pdfs/Danin-refl.pdf

[38] https://www.shroud.com/iannone.pdf

[39] https://earlychurchhistory.org/christian-symbols/why-pollen-on-the-shroud-of-turin-proves-it-is-real/

[40] https://www.shroud.com/iannone.pdf

[41] https://www.shroud.com/guscin.htm

[42] https://www.shroud.com/pdfs/FilascoinsJune1982.pdf

[43] http://theshroudofturin.blogspot.com/2013/05/the-shroud-of-turin-26-other-marks-5.html

[44] Dr Alan Whanger- coins on eyes/ similarities to other pictures of Christ

https://www.youtube.com/watch?v=-MTDN_2PI4I

[45] http://www.ohioshroudconference.com/papers/p24.pdf

[46]   http://shroud3d.com/findings/three-hebrew-letters-on-surface-of-solid-object

[47] https://www.shroud.com/78conclu.htm

[48] the Shroud of Turin- a case for authenticity- Rev. Fr. Vittorio Guerrera

[49] https://www.shroud.com/pdfs/ohiomaloneypaper.pdf

https://www.shroud.com/meacham.htm

[50] The Tablet-June 2015- Louise Cowley

https://louisecowley.wordpress.com/the-shroud-of-turin-2/

[51] https://www.ncbi.nlm.nih.gov/pmc/articles/PMC5493404/

[52] William Meacham preserves this story in his book 'The Rape of the Turin Shroud. '(Lulu, 2005)

[53] http://triablogue.blogspot.com/2014/04/the-1982-carbon-dating-of-shroud-of.html

The Resurrection Of The Shroud [New York, New York: M. Evans and Company, 2000], n. 30 on 304.

THE SHROUD: THE EVIDENCE

Printed in Great Britain
by Amazon

28086814R00083